THE SUN KING

THE
SUN KING

CONOR
O'CALLAGHAN

WAKE FOREST

UNIVERSITY PRESS

FOR MARY VIRGINIA

This life:
We get old enough and finally really like it!

THE SUN KING

LORDSHIP

He assembled a console inside the stable's glass doors
and had his narrator come this close to banging
his own mother in half-light in the late '70s.

Rabbits tripped the halogen from the courtyard's hay.
He was still smoking, memorizing Burns by a hearth,
singing to flicked embers that looked soluble in its black.

The antique Nokia on the butcher block in the bathroom
vibrated at all hours like tropical wildlife.
Whitewashed horsehair plaster shed magnolia petals.

Whatever glare each fresh day uploaded
made a disco-ball in the double-glazing's exterior smash
and blissed splinters of violet all over the upstairs.

Fuelled on pre-paid credit and Finnish cider
and love like Technicolor flooding the bloodstream
he had heard tell of before but never dreamt,

he sprinted nightly to the sweet shop in Riverstown
and cracked up twice in one week when the lottery scanner
bleated 'Not a Winner' and shot the breeze

with teenage freckles skitting on the warmth
and caught scraps of signal overspilling the north
and left times on your voicemail from a bank of poppies

and thistle in that field down to the sea grown fallow
with pre-historic agricultural hardware
like Coney Island rides *entre deux guerres*

and sipped green tea as if it were chlorophyll and filled
a Borders tote and struck out on the rush of feeling in flight,
flying beneath the radar. You know what he's like.

Oestrous, cock-struck, you tubed first thing from A to B,
Vivienne Westwood number pilling at the seams,
to the garden flat he'd blagged that had a suntrap at the back.

Once, then, your head hitting the top bunk's slats,
a teaspoon of colostrum squeezed onto his tongue.
Once later on on the patio upright against a wall

amid calls home and spliffs with liquorice skins
and rocket fetched from a stall on Primrose Hill.
Once in stagnant water in grey dark in the bath.

Twice on the square of two mattresses dragged together,
missionary, all fours, dried clots showered away at dawn.
Once on lino behind a sofa glued to *Charlie and Lola*.

Three years after the Kings Cross bomb to the minute
was silence you were underground for and missed.
It's pissing on Belfast City's solitary terminal,

he buzzed to tell you and got lost in the patchy coverage
of Hope Valley your express was chuntering east of
and heard next to nothing the guts of August.

There's no return route, is there? You sussed that too?
The truth, much as time does, vanishes behind.
It's not like userdata, waiting retrieval by us.

I ran low on juice on the dual carriageway south
that narrowed to a dirt track dead-ending at aftergrass
where the house no longer stood

and the bay had retreated into its shell of cloud
and real estate signs were popping along the coast
like crocus bulbs come late to flowering

or speech bubbles in some dumb graphic novel
that sees its hero's profile boot corrupt
and earth laid waste in the interstices between realms.

Forgive me. I couldn't hack the secrecy any more
than I could go on outsourcing what history we share
to the chum-of-a-chum third party beard above

that's kidding no one. I couldn't breathe between it,
the 'you' you truly were and spaced, benighted me
already sentimental for the future's blown cover.

Forgive the ruse. Forgive my coming clean.
It can still be a secret, lover, ours and ours alone.
This is its safest keeping: nobody's going to see it.

AMONG OTHER THINGS

The rest have
driven to the mall.
Any second now
will be too dark.

This close to the edge,
among other things,
I read.

Leaves rattle overhead.
Little pockets
of canned applause
sift through
the screened porch
in next door's yard.

WILD STRAWBERRIES

Saturday, late
and but for a handful
of neighbourhood girls
hanging in the street,
nothing doing.

I cut the back,
brim the yard-cart.
The air is thick
with the scent
of wild strawberries'
mown flesh.

This weather we keep
the bedroom sash ajar.
I lie to myself:
they're not metaphors.
They are not metaphors.

SWELL

Mid-March, on the daily a.m. drop-off
through a bunch of affluent side streets
between school and here

a refrigerated dairy produce truck
keeps catching almond and dogwood branches,
so much that blossoms blizzard

the windscreen and moonroof
and I have to switch the wipers
to intermittent in its slipstream.

All I mean to say is that it was lovely,
that not every given is bleak or wrong
and some even are as gorgeous as they are elementary.

The kids come home on different buses
the same shade of egg yolk.
We call my mother from the shore for Easter.

That truck and blossoms story gets longer,
hokier, with each retelling. I'm not bothered.
April's bright stretches, the mailman says, are swell.

Our local 'Y' widens its opening hours a smidgen.
The clay courts opposite pock and shuffle.
I learn to swim.

LANTERN SLIDES

Time was Money
                    stopped with us upwards
                                        of a month
            once every year   lording it large
        burning hard   both ends.
            A daylight hoot   by night
    the fridge shuddered   supplements rustled
            and there Money always
        already was all palaver all
                            sugary waffle.
What memory prospers
                        in grain it spends in pixels
You still happen   on receipts secreted
        about the place like flutter
            slips or eggs at Easter.
Cuckoospit, chlorophyll?
                    Sure thing . . . Spring
spells mostly those gorgeous residual
                            jitters borne of assessment
of a self that used be
                pretty fiscal. This
        is of the carpet
                    bag Money never returned for,
a parallelogram of vivid dust through the screen door.
This is
        of an heirloom bound in cloth Atlantic Calm.
This is of
            a note unopened between shakers on the table that
        (till now) remained implicit. Don't even
        dream about it.

TIGER REDUX

Tiger, tiger, word of mouth
now that you've gone AWOL, south,
has it you were lame or wrong,
sleaze incarnate all along.

Truth? Though you were mighty strange—
so *laissez faire*, so *keep the change*—
spare us from the dope who (bore)
digs the hole we were before.

In the forests of the past
burns your blinding sun, the blast,
cat's pyjamas, rush we'd ('craic')
gladly have you magic back.

Magic back designer shakes,
gold-soaked morning-after flakes,
fibre optics, soft-top wheels,
tax incentive movie stills,

Xerox plants like pleasure domes,
sushi bars, the second homes,
investment apts in Budapest,
light rail lanes, the glitz, the rest.

Magic back the casual flings'
appetite for matter/things,
owning/craving all at once,
one point three for tea and buns

served off Polish number plates,
syndicates, the real estates
pre being repossessed by ghosts,
bubbly snipes and server hosts

bobbing up like crèche balloons,
cranes, Nigerian gospel tunes
whooping out of refuge blocks,
jet-set enclaves, shares and stocks

crashing every christening bash,
laundry bags grown used to cash,
polished granite firmaments,
sleeplessness and supplements

a glossy weekend dawns to, warms,
films of sweat that habit forms,
pins-and-needles, sales agreed,
decades on skip-forward, speed,

adrenalin like lemon zest,
murmurs, furniture distressed,
bouncy castles hard with air,
clubs, arrhythmic ticks, the blare

of sirens' song on motorways
overheating into haze.
Seems we were (regret sublime?)
at the party all the time.

All that *jouissance*, that juice.
Post the '80s outpost blues
(signed away and midweek pushed),
all that feeling central, flushed.

All that buzz like year-round Springs.
All that North Atlantic bling's
rising tide, its waves and boom
charging in an empty room.

All that hub became us rich:
all euphoric debt, all itch.
All that sweetness, green stuff love
couldn't furnace fast enough.

MID TO UPPER SEVENTIES

He rests *The Narrow Road to the Deep North*
on an arm of the sunroom sofa-bed.
He walks to the front
to change the AC setting.

His father is asleep on the floor
before the hearth of a gas fire
that has gathered cobwebs since March.
Val Doonican, muted, is rocking on TV.

The year is now.
The house is forty miles or so
south of the Virginia line.
He hasn't seen his father,
spoken with him, in at least a decade.
Jimmy Carter was governor of Georgia
when Val's one-man slot came on the air.

He goes back in the sunroom.
Neither Val nor his dad will be there
when next he walks out front.
The book has fallen face-down on the oak
and it takes him a really long time,
years in fact, to recover his place.

NINETEEN SEVENTY-SIX

Our superior has gone on a reconnaissance mission
to one of the hospitality tents the Open lays on for suits.
Pending further orders, we are to man the tenth tee.

The symbolism of where we stand—the midway mark,
its dry breeze turned back into, its music faced—
is still a fraction conceptual for our frame of reference.

We are communicating thus to resemble astronauts.
Whenever a threeball of little consequence drifts past,
an ageing life-form holds aloft a vertical QUIET PLEASE.

Our mother is visiting an acquaintance from pre-history
whose husband has a name which echoes 'cinnamon',
a limp from international squash and something terminal.

I pray that my freckles will amalgamate into a tan.
Galleries erupt out on the links like flares or galaxies
imploding above our heads. The dunes are singed to beige.

I pray for Demis Roussos who eats two ducks a day;
for the weatherman who has only to toss dandelions
nightly onto the twenty-six counties and hope they stick.

WOODSMOKE

I buy this woodstove
('Big Boy', Birmingham, AL)
    in a clearance sale
for the hut we're fixing up
at the top of the garden.

    For weeks all three-legs,
twenty-rusting-bucks of it
    hogs the patio.
It looks like some wild creature
in from the sticks to hunt scraps.

    Stock reports double
as tinder, TV listings,
    twigs the ice storm left
in its wake, war coverage
and a struck match. Flames bob up

    the split hotplate's cleft
like starlings newly hatched.
    I feed logs enough
to burn longer than I'll stand
and dawn blanches the embers.

    A month of woodsmoke.
The wardrobe reeks charred resin.
    The kids think I'm nuts:
their own hobo—duffel coat,
travel mug—states out the line.

Times I'll hum to it,
tell it stuff. It changes me,
       much as it changes
maple and newsprint to dust
gauzing porches, drifting blocks

       toward the highway,
the mall's afterglow, the sky.
       It halves the fallow
stretch from Xmas to Spring's boom.
Then the fire marshal stops by.

       It doesn't matter.
Since Daylight Savings happened
       the neighbours can rest.
Becoming is what matters,
the passage, the whetted axe.

       I get an odd peace
imagining these clear nights
       how bits of spare cash,
Alabama, this garden,
my son's and daughter's faces

       at the sliding door,
the market's ebbs, the stacked dead,
       a hut placed on pause,
its stove's words, my writing them,
the page's threshold even,

this book in your hand,
the bookstore open Sunday
    in which you're reading,
are all bound to get threaded
through some flame's liminal eye.

IN PRAISE OF SPRINKLERS

Heat, the shadow of a cypress tree . . .
        Spring resembles
a crossword left unfinished on a stoop
        while *sassafras*
        gets looked up,
a steam engine trembling the distance,
        an empty glass.
Each afternoon survives your absence.
Elsewhere the lived world happens
        and thunder rumbles
above those worse ways than this to be.

Go. We are seldom quite so missed
        as we suppose.
See through the sunspots that the murk
        of a shuttered store
        implies. The paintwork
softens, the beech leaves' reflection
        chats to the screen door,
the umpteenth azure dome in succession
rolls over choosing its sleeping position,
        the grass grows
minutely and the path dries. I insist.

TRANSLATION

Imagine you are this poem
moments before it is translated,

full of old stuff nobody says anymore.
There is a mill wheel. There is even a soul,

for crying out loud! And there is this stile
you sit out on to catch the last of a sun

that will not survive from the original
when it happens as something

really simple like kids moving in
to the affluent block parallel to this.

They have been playing lacrosse in the heat.
The trucks have come and gone.

Now they are placing down their sticks.
Now they are standing gawping through

that gap in the hedge the cats bored
years ago as if through fog.

The farmyard implements
scattered like punctuation marks,

the armless tailor's dummy in the asparagus,
have no equivalents in their tongue.

They cannot hear or answer the woodpecker's
landline ringing out in your maple.

They have only the handful of phrases
you are mouthing to go on.

I have a soul, you appear to be calling.
Make of my soul what you will.

THE SUN KING

I wanted his sky-blue Ford, its sheetrock, its transmission issues.
I listened to his low-down yodelling skimming sunk studs
and snake rattles like wind chimes round his mantle in the hills
and parables waiting for windows to arrive where some lunchbox
was always asked what sort of lunchbox he took Roy for.
Le roi soleil.
 It stuck, from first coming with a bucket of mud
to the day of reckoning his lady friend brought marble cake
and Roy joined hands in a ring that all lost rooms be filled
by a sun to which even the godless among us could say Amen.

Then one afternoon *Leaves of Grass* fell onto the laminate.
The station wagon wasn't in the drive. The sprinklers,
for all the gilt and shadow in the street, had run dry.
My boy and girl were grown elsewhere. And somehow I,
five years east, woke in mind of an odd-job deity no heathen
need ever wake in mind of. King of sun, pray for me again.

A NEST OF TABLES

1

Consider all those vanities, extendable Danish oak veneers,
Breton refectory longboats, canasta drop-leafs, rustic trestles
you bespeak & grieve & to this day measure eras by, years.
Consider all those truces opposing handlebar moustaches,
greatcoats, trusses, may never have struck in field tents
but for whatever taboret or oval drum happened to hand.
Consider peace, its news, its plusses pealing between hamlets:
woods not cut, wheat not flattened, walls for once not manned.

2

The thing about things, surfaces,
the ache ingrained in bric-a-brac
is the way that each refuses
point blank to miss us back.

3

I could use
a   sunrise

THE SERVER ROOM

Even now there are floors where a blue skies
thinktank is thanking its lucky stats,
calendarizing all foreseeable windows,
disassembling beneath into Easter's
veritable orangery of hols.

Late evening—a relatively complex
complex of plate glass, workstations idle
but for process in situ, mail arriving—
oversees elements of good practice.
One has no charge to answer. The report said.

An auction site that shall remain nameless-
ly logged into pops one final alert.
Its watchlist's portable Olivetti
(vintage, aquamarine, some signs of use)
is ticking down in red, has been outbid.

There they blow, on the sandstone esplanade,
the gods, the designated parking bays,
barn conversions in the Peaks, wishing well,
whose minuted peaches soon as tabled
spray through local cable in bullet form.

Let the auction fallow. Folly it was,
a romance of keys that goosepimple pages,
of carriages returning with a chink
of light relief and with no memory
to speak of. Leave it grey out. Click Refresh.

Loaves and fishes in the beverage dock
surplus to the shindig for a dray horse
drifting out to grass; swipe-card/lanyard lost;
Morris dancers monthly in the atrium
embedding a culture of celebration

of natural wastage, adapting to scale;
drop-in sessions at the multi-faith centre;
calls for papers 'Theorizing Normalcy
& the Mundane'; donations to a present
tense defecting for the private sector,

and ripe in bold like fruit unpicked in briar
a sent-from-BlackBerry 'wish you were there'
where *there*'s a chichi Hoxton tapas dive
or that low-tide sandbar from Whitstable
through the Channel they euphemize The Street…

Such gorgeous nubless hubris! Source of which,
a door unmarked this side of History,
becomes a bonnet bee, a bugaboo
at hours like these with all one's colleagues split
and thirsts for loveknots slaked and spirits drab,

and below in sun the tram to Halfway
through the current plan, the ring road
chock-a-block with external stakeholders,
dominant drivers, opinion formers,
appropriate partners and other 'friends'.

Refresh. And lo! it lands, good news, on cue:
the gospel according to the apostles
of policy, their interim review
via ribbons of white Vatican smoke
or bargeloads towed on virtual canal,

words like the shadows of dirigibles
inching over the closest horizon,
lambs' wolves, bright wolds and dales of old flannel
refurbished for uncertain ages,
great folds of hosannas, angelic notes

all sung suds and bubbles as in some
luxury shower foam infomercial
their mission and vision of pastoral,
maintenance/enhancement of the estate,
emergent patterns, developing fields,

provision for 'real life' experience,
husbandry in selected areas,
arias of a solitary central host
delivered to us from in excelsis,
a class of listserv lesser doxology,

our offer's lingua franca reaped and baled
in the graces, airs, of summer's grammar,
green shoots, brand evolution, new markets,
the ale froth of quality, management,
such sumptuous fluff, acres of the stuff,

heavenly bouffant meringues of language,
focus and progression, hope's woolly vowels
working closely with the opalescence
of systems, the knowledge economy,
its argot's luminous opacity

like upholstered immaculate plumage
blooming off brewed hops out towards Burbage,
the remote mother-of-pearl cumulus
of such institutional verbiage
one still finds something oddly moving in.

Refresh. There's nothing left to send/receive.
The cooler is swamped by a ring of empties,
the gridlock seconded to a stream in spate.
The time is now, its last abiding brief
to click upon the happening night without.

Refresh. Now's as pure as any chance
to retrace contraflow the current ocean-bound.
Ascend in clear segments of fluorescence,
past clusters of furniture for chilled confabs,
partitioned space's bureaucratic murk.

Be sure to check there's no one else around.
Then make that door unmarked an echo chamber
to drown the churning of a copy job
resumed from lord knows when, a tripping bus,
the draught's conditional honour of bliss

and listen hard. This interior's hiss
of dehumidifiers, fans and ohms
coursing through each missive's chosen font,
of tangled vines of ampersands, of fronds
of ethernet mycelium/ports,

it rises at that murmurous force ahead,
the rumour blessèd precious few have heard
and fewer glimpsed, a falls at altitude
that pilgrims — handfuls, barefoot, far between,
in search of altered states — give credence to.

Behold the server and the server's place
of worship's working templates. Praise the here
where mountains float above a pea-soup mist
and all that blue skies thinking has been saved.
Pray to the deities of eternal code. Refresh.

Up here on the lam, the limb of oneself,
form a cup of digits/palms and wait
for data like rain meltwater cold
to pool to brimming point, to cascade down.
Drink. Be whole again beyond communication.

COMMA

Infinite
blip that
a flyover
sped beneath
scores into
a down-

pour on the
soft-top's
timpani is
somewhere I
could stop
indefinitely . . .

PEACE

There's got to be a term in currency for this:
the debt all losses owe to sentiment
for loss that wakes in happiness; a grief-
nostalgia some Germanic compound coins
and we don't share. A shadow warms to peace.
The heatwave, at its stillest, yearns a storm.

It's not unlike the ache to feel betrayed,
that farthest shore that lovers love towards.
They bus it there one cloudless afternoon
of trust and hope, and paddle knee-deep gold,
and find a bar, and hitchhike back the road
a little sunstruck, little lost for words.

Word is, they've had it bankrolling Arcadia.
The goatherd gods have cancelled half the milk
and grazed their flocks beyond the sell-by date.
The virtual troops are posting flags on loose
Cycladic change. The honey's come unstuck,
its bubbles blown away in dark. Today —

a public holiday lie-in, no alarm;
the charge in limbs and juice desire exacts
from dawn; a snooze; a courtyard's azure glass;
her inch-of-water wartime bath, on me;
the numbers our transistor bleats — might be
remembered as the first forgetful acts.

THE BULK COLLECTION

Those shapes
the sidewalk furnishes

its darks with—
that's a soda fountain

and that
a chaise longue—

are like synonyms
for letting go

I look up.
I love 'relinquish',

its starry black:
I wake too soon

to the rooms I am
to mind till May

reciting its psalm
for forced air.

THE HIGH ROAD

Game Three moves west
to the Rockies
and drags to all hours.

I go room to room
flicking off power points.
Nothing is there,
except the snowy
edges of mountains
of boxes.

The moon's light
must be worn out.
It has come so far!
It should get ale, bread,
aired linen turned down.

EMERGENCY

This Tecsun transistor propped
among lavender pots and hostas
                                buzzes close-of-trading stats
swamped by the corner house frying out.

Since March's cloudbursts
                            drops seeped under
the laminated yard-sign shrine
to their eldest camouflage his face

with freckles like coppers in a salsa jar.
Every time a teller
                        tips them in her scales
they are rust scraps of some GI carrier
come unstuck in Free State fog

                                    the week of Dresden

from which the old man's oldest
drinking crony looted a charred Zippo
that flicks petals to this day
with the *tricolore*   of one

blown from the gingko over my head
onto a mountain track where Bashō suffers
the entreaties of two fallen concubines.

Imagine the pewter approaching sunrise.
Yesterday was an angry sea.
                              Tomorrow
will be wisteria vines far off the beaten path.

Follow, by all means, if you must.
This goes only one direction
and we are veering years from a return.

THE PILOT LIGHT

Every night the spare cylinder's yellow
has shone in the bathroom window
like one of those lopsided moons
hanging out over Clare,
that stray's bray carried thirty Augusts
and the island's intermittent pinhead
run aground on day.
There have been afternoons
when the white manes flattened
and even the cement out front
was warm underfoot.
I'm leaving the gate stoned back,
the pilot light budding in your name.
Is it safe? Sure, and I like what it says.

REQUIRED FIELDS

They can be timothy, these miscellaneous
undulating pewters we keep returning to.
Up to a certain point, they can be a breeze.

The number and month between 'Hey Jude'
and the student riots that a corridor in El Paso
was filled with yelps on your behalf? No sweat.

A combination of the last four digits in a line
long disconnected and the name of the border terrier
that met its maker under an artic? At a stretch . . .

But this? This is one memory too far, the reliquary
of an anorak's afternoon mislaid doodling cul-de-sacs
for halfwits who omit to save on record all the facts —

such as you. It's getting on. The last red asterisk
has begun to shine. Perhaps at times it's better
to submit to the pin-drop of forgetfulness,

accept that there are questions of provenance
no amount of empty boxes can hope to answer,
leave the past to time itself back to a Square One.

Ours is stored this weather
in outsized plywood cubes in a warehouse
off one of the ring road's quieter exits.

We Mapquest to it, postcode to postcode,
a Grade A grey day the kids are still at grammar
and sift the flotsam of an old life shipped ahead.

None of it translates. The antiques mall maple,
the see-through tubs of Crocs and Cargoes,
belong to a blank we are moved too far from now to fill.

A chap from Blackpool who works the forklift
ushers us into the office for something warm.
His mother always swore that she'd go back

and he ferries the Kawasaki over twice a year.
First night he likes to climb the scarp,
three sheets to the dark, and shut the turbo off.

We sit there nursing Typhoo and plastic bags.
This side of the water, whenever he can't sleep,
he stocktakes stars above the Turf Road, the Windy Gap.

SOSPESO

They've this tipple
in Napoli
you stand and leave
unpoured weeks, years

and some shade calls
in off the skids.
What's not to love?
The thought that is

we hold as we
hope to one day
one another,
like family:

the awning-scrolled
glow-swayed-out-of
molten tumbler
amber of this

tealight tilting
slantwise (if you
say so) in our
suspended name.

DIVISION STREET

April's Wednesdays see you two-thirds home.
The chlorophyll, the *joie de vivre*
of grief this justified's
too sweet to flip
or bluff.

We live through fractions thus, conceptualize
each met reserve as apples, pies.
The season's coolest app
for three-way splits
is love

and gets recalled. The grass is dappled by branches
of Starbucks, Boots, the beergarden black.
The evening turns out chrome.
Division Street,
end of.

I tweet your vanishing trick across the green
this happy hour of every week
when you are lime in leaf
and I am sap
enough

to carve your footfalls up like auction lots:
the ring road lights, the skyline blues,
that button I all but feel
beneath your thumb
buzz off.

What planet, baby, did you say you're on?
And what am I bid this third alone
of birds and vintage shops
for buying back
your leave?

THE UNFAITHFUL HOUSEWIFE

Then I led her to the river
certain she was still a virgin
though she had a husband.
The fourth Friday in July,
as good as on a promise.
The street lights were vanishing
and the crickets flaring up.
Last bend out of town
I brushed her sleepy breasts.
They blossomed of a sudden
like the tips of hyacinths
and the starch of her petticoat
bustled in my ear like silk
slit by a dozen blades.
The pines, minus their halo
of silver, grew huger
and the horizon of dogs
howled a long way from the river.

Past the blackberry bushes,
the rushes and whitethorn,
beneath her thatch of hair,
I made a dip in the sand.
I took off my neckerchief.
She unstrapped her dress,
me my gun and holster,
she her layers of slips . . .
Not tuberose, not shell,
has skin half as smooth

nor does mirror glass
have half the shimmer.
Her hips flitted from me
like a pair of startled perch:
the one full of fire,
the other full of cold.
That night I might
as well have ridden
the pick of the roads
on a mother-of-pearl mare
without bridle or stirrups.
Gentleman that I am,
I won't say back the scraps
she whispered to me.
It dawned out there
to leave my lip bitten.
Filthy with soil and kisses,
I led her from the river
and the spears of lilies
battled in the air.

I behaved only the way
a blackguard like me behaves.
I offered her a big creel
of hay-coloured satins.
I had no wish to fall for her.
She has a husband after all,
though she was still a virgin
when I led her to the river.

Federico García Lorca, 'La Casada Infiel'

THE END OF THE LINE

is a pressure gauge touching red, running empty. Tap the Enter key and — there!
— a solidus of light is thrown across your path from the balcony above.
It helps to think of some fat lute shod in espadrilles. It helps to sing of love,
between each blip whereby your song excuses itself to the cool night air.
It should get to feel like those seconds following sex, their little death
made littler still by missed beats just like that and the fear that all oxygen is gone
halfway down the next and you're bound for that plot the muses call 'Anon'.
You're not. Relax. Thank your lucky stars they're full of stops to catch your breath.

This is how I learned. In shallows cordoned off for paddling and kids, I found
it took the baker's dozen sideways sucks to tip the far wall and come back
it takes to say a sonnet whole. I climb a lane, balloon my lungs to the diaphragm
(where did the balcony go? where did you? where has this pool arrived from?)
and fall too hard for that point of no return where the water looms deep and black.
This is when it comes: drained of noise, night without rungs, no lifeguards round.

40

REVISION

The Street acquires a name while you are gone.
Sunset, Queen, or maybe the intersection
between them you could not picture first time round
and sidle through one evening lately

while a Latina paints her shingle plum. See?
There is always time. Even those times
when there are no lights on inside and the key jams
and every draughty room has been repossessed.

Then the best revision is starting over,
much as a fall of unblemished snow
from that system the weather channel's satellite
billows all day towards you across the state.

Only, snow does not know, you know,
its asterisks have long been ground to dust.
You just have to take it with a pinch
of the salt they are gritting on the roads

while you mark your place and I talk on.
See, again. The back yard is black at first.
The white stray mewls for a fistful of 9Lives
somewhere past your landlord's midden.

If this is immortality, let it slide.
The chicken coop fades up, the boundary fence.
There is still hope, even now,
and for all those light years shining overhead.

KINGDOM COME

FOR VONA

That Arts & Crafts house still for sale,
shutters all always shut,

is the safest place to park.
Blaming the market, they shipped north.

Who'd have thought a year
would find me stalking our old selves

while neighbours wheel their trash
to the sidewalk for the morning?

Mostly I mark papers
by light run off the alternator.

Though lately I've been praying, lady,
that whatever kingdom come there is

is a street we owned a place on
where the life we meant to love

and ran screaming from mid-stream
completes itself without us

and it's evening over and over again.
A piece of Plantation House chandelier

is dismantling the last bar of sun
into bit and bobs of iris.

In the yard each lost wish still chimes
even though there's no wind.

There is a barometer stalled on 'Fair',
a slow air remastered on the squeezebox.

The sea, gone miles out of its way, is there
as a screensaver reflected in the screendoor.

And our heirs are there in the ping-pong
and hip-hop of the garage's murk.

And I, in some shape or form,
am there as well. And you are there.

BORDERS

Its closing got mixed up in my head.
Today's Sunday. Sundays are nine.
Doors were locked, inside deserted,
but for two Latino cleaning ladies.

I sat a bit in the parking bay.
Fresh Air was rerunning this barrier—
a real thing, not a symbol—
from Tijuana across to the Gulf.

They looked beautiful in there,
laughing, dusting books in silhouette,
and maybe their beauty was part, yes,
of being this far from home.

We're between moons all weekend.
I tuned over to bluegrass on the road.
A hand waved from the security box
and I waited for the boom.

GAME NIGHT

Love not
being in the loop.

Grant the spruces' wish,
the golf compound
graying out of use,
SUVs in the IT lot,
power outage,
a chorus from the quad.

Bless the elsewhere
where others are
not here or you.

And rain
after midnight . . .
Ask yourself,
is that rain or bells?

JANUARY DROUGHT

It needn't be tinder, this juncture of the year,
a cigarette flicked from car to brush.

The woods' parchment is given
to cracking asunder the first puff of wind.
Yesterday a big sycamore came across First
and Hawthorne and is there yet.

The papers say it has to happen,
if just as dribs and drabs on the asbestos siding.
But tonight is buckets of stars as hard and dry as dimes.

A month's supper things stacks in the sink.
Tea brews from water stoppered in the bath
and any thirst carried forward is quenched thinking you,
piece by piece, an Xmas gift hidden
and found weeks after: the ribbon, the box.

I have reservoirs of want enough
to freeze many nights over.

GRAVITY

That light dusting
on the arch to Lucky Palace
is a thing of the past.

Initialize a windscreen
on Newton St: the letters fill
in same increments by which
the afternoon assesses its gravity.
The casino doorman is catching his chips.

Three equals remission. Feels years
since the text alert did
its impression of crashing cymbals.
The loft above is running *Six Feet Under*—
the box-set, sounds like—on a loop.
Back of the art museum a van bangs.

Four, and it's coming
down in spades.

THREE SIX FIVE ZERO

I called up Tech and got the voicemail code.
It's taken me this long to find my feet.
Since last we spoke that evening it has snowed.

Fifty-four new messages. Most are old
and blinking into a future months complete.
I contacted Tech to get my voicemail code

to hear your voice, not some bozo on the road
the week of Thanksgiving dubbing me his sweet
and breaking up and bleating how it snowed

the Nashville side of Chattanooga and slowed
the beltway to a standstill. The radio said sleet.
The kid in Tech sent on my voicemail code.

I blew a night on lightening the system's load,
woke to white enveloping the trees, the street
that's blanked out by my leaving. It had snowed.

Lately others' pasts will turn me cold.
I heard out every message, pressed delete.
I'd happily forget my voice, the mail, its code.
We spoke at last that evening. Then it snowed.

THE PEARL WORKS

may this song leave
darkness alone

Say one of these a week: a couplet, maxed-out tweet. Sound twee?
Resolve. The year has gone ahead, the bytes are disappearing. Follow me.

o

Little Yang Sing, Yuzu, Hunan, Wong Wong, Imperial Siam:
all those bright syllables cascading into the bottle-bank at 5 a.m.

o

Winter singles, my luminous son, glare so gold it could be Flushing Meadows:
facing out of is serving 3-D slowmo, into is receiving shadows.

o

Year of the Dragon & red gooseberry lanterns & a prepaid minutes stall.
My mam IMs all hours: 'They're getting northern lights off Donegal!'

o

50

Lent

Spring. We get it.
After weeks on ice, buckets of pussy willow outside Woo Sang blossom & each evening is granted a little
extra credit.

○

Half-term home. Who knew post-boom would be (excuse me) sublime?
Ghost estates, cranes paused, office block shells, pubs dead like wartime . . .

○

The wedge of poplar driftwood fetched at low tide at Clogherhead?
Why that driftwood's now my bathroom doorstop in Chinatown. Gotta love it!

○

Glory be the carnal surface:
aluminium on flats across, blasted lime by late sun; the water cooler's translucence a still p.m. in the office.

○

This is the goose-egg symbol of perfection that your perfectly pursed little lips mouthed in my direction,
darling, many many moons ago.

O . . . .

○

And this? The handful of coppers daylight borrows from October.
Come bright hour. Be bright. Be ours. Be extra, ecstatic, immaterial, other.

○

The three days

Friday as good as any & dim sum buffets heaving. My pearl comes with a side of nights
that are tropical, equatorial even, tossed in sweats.

○

Easter

It's harder to usher a banker into heaven than it's to thread a zeppelin,
say, through the eye of the invisible middle syllable of 'Dublin'.

○

You hear that? A city united all afternoon in a chorus of field breaths.
'Refresh,' the buffering May wind says, 'refresh refresh refresh . . .'

○

I will build my love a bower by yon clear and crystal fountain
And all around the bower I will pile flowers of the mountain

○

Friggin' Wigan pier! Nada here, zilch, squat, divil the peep. . . . .
'The point's the *road* to Wigan pier,' she's giggling, 'not the pier.' Deep.

○

Sun king, king of evening gold, forgive me being this spaced.
Forgive me all this solitude I love. Forgive me all the life I have misplaced.

○

It was February all June. It was raining and it was going to rain.
The blocked bard & sa muse anglaise amused themselves in the Royal Marine.

○

Midsummer leaps too early. July already. Someone, place on frame-by-frame, on pause, these long days.
Hey! The pearl works. It really does.

○

Herewith my current credo: all pastoral is virtual, ever was & shall be, world without end … Boom!
This day of Our Lord I glimpsed into the server room.

○

Something bucolic to bureaucracy in high season: its clock stopped on four,
its skeletal staff refectory, its dried mail, its deserted corridor.

○

I sleep in my daughter's bed one night, I sleep in my son's the next.
I pray that I will wake each morning to azure, to absolution, to text.

o

Another gold, another 'send her victorious', another August bank holiday . . .
Cue the heavens' candyfloss, the carvery lunch, the cor anglais.

o

'A Survey of Post-Colonialism: Some Introductory Remarks': The switch in 1995 from 'Bombay' to 'Mumbai',
I must admit, rather passed me by.

o

Glory be the last of summer's ambrosia:
spate ale; beeswax evening cumulus; a drove of heifers in single file on a footbridge over the M42.

o

Now not even lonesomeness, they crow, is subject for the muse.
Tell that to crossroads. Tell that to a bullfrog's mating call in rushes. Tell that to the blues.

o

I toast my new age. I drink its tongue-roll, its wheel-whirr, on the road to Montecarlo.
Quarantaquattro, quarantaquattro, quarantaquattro . . .

o

Grazie Signore for ordinary time, for this privilege of sound & light,
for bricks & stones that hold its heat after the sun has been & set.

o

Come, Summer. Your freckle weather's gone too far. It's October!
Fill a barrow of olive logs. Call in the coppers March borrowed. Give over.

o

The castanets—nay, this maraca (singular)—a fistful of pistachio shells in the compost tub is a bitch to play in time with anything else.

○

Funny the way it is that you can confirm 'friends' that are virtual and yet solitude still comes exclusively in a form that's far too real.

○

A curse:
on the Tuscan Elmer Fudds this morning popping songbirds. May skylark, woodcock, thrush ghosts rain like locusts upon their house.

○

Glory be this glare, this solar self, this blanched out screen.
Glory be its tangerine charging me all afternoon. Glory be its indoor green.

○

For the record I've adored a solemn O, its whiff of silicon,
the incremental polonaise a copper coil unspools, the windfall bronze I cycle on.

○

The table's turning still. For the record, I've collected discs of icy sun,
including its sulphur-sleeved deluxe edition lemon vinyl dawn.

○

I love the way a reflection so strong can singe a spot into your field of vision
like the tiny corona of a frozen lake that you've just wizzed on.

○

The German market's black. Another year has had it bar the shouting,
bar the downward spiral's blaze that (blinded) we go out in.

○

Dawn. Here's hoping the Mayans were on the wacky backy when they made that call.
Open the drivers of another cycle's sun, select Run→Install.

○

This world . . . We get older & find it grows less hard.
Last night I dreamt that we were back at the Mystik Gas on Cascade & Shady Boulevard.

○

Grazie Signore for the sacraments of stuff: lamé throws, saffron,
seagrass needles, shepherd's huts (bespoke) we blow the year's remainder surfing.

○

Grazie Signore for this fathomless astronomical fluke of landing here at all,
for the full circle that we've come, the blast it's been, the ball . . .

○

59

I saw the danger, yet I walked along the enchanted way,
And I said, let grief be a fallen leaf at the dawning of the day

O

O slow coach, freeze-mode yellow solar yoyo O hand-thrown old gold snow globe
O rose most blown O whole whorled 'out there' lodestar *de l'aube*

O

O glory hole *l'aurore* O bowl-of-cored-sloes stone-cold low glow
O homophone O grown son showboating solo over our known world so moments ago

O

O heliotrope O blossom bole O trompe l'oeil orange grove we home in
O old soul, no bones glowworm without whose strobe we'd mope eternal gloaming

O

O closing words O lovely hopeless song (one more!) invoking love gone south
O storeroom door that's on a slope & opens outwards O open mouth

60

NOTES AND ACKNOWLEDGMENTS

The epigraph is from "The Sweat" by Gary Snyder. "Revision" appears in *Peter Fallon: Poet, Publisher, Translator, Editor* (Irish Academic Press, 2013, edited by Richard Russell), and is dedicated to Peter. "The Server Room" incorporates several external texts, especially the "Refreshed Corporate Plan" of Sheffield Hallam University and "Directive" by Robert Frost. It has previously appeared as an e-chapbook from Smithereens Press, thanks to Kenneth Keating. "Translation" was written for a former student, Emily Mihalik, who is hearing impaired.

"The Pearl Works", named after a derelict nineteenth-century cutlery factory in Sheffield city centre, is selected and revised from a Twitter page: a sequence of improvised couplets of exactly 140 characters, one for every week of 2012. The current selection, dedicated to Paul Durcan, appeared as a chapbook from New Fire Tree Press, thanks to David Devanny. Its epigraph is from *Tape for the Turn of the Year* by A. R. Ammons. Those italicized song lyrics are from, respectively, "Wild Mountain Thyme" by Francis McPeake and "On Raglan Road" by Patrick Kavanagh. Many of the later entries were posted from San Martino in Colle, Lucca, thanks to Sophie Siemens and David Adolphe.

Thanks also to the Poetry Foundation for the Bess Hokin Prize of 2007, and to An Chomhairle Ealaíon/The Arts Council of Ireland for a bursary in 2011/12.

I would like to thank others whose example and friendship have been important: Vona Groarke, David Wheatley, Justin Quinn, Eamon Little, John McAuliffe, Gerard Fanning, Ralph Black, Jim Hans, Rachel Genn and Mary Peace, to whom this book is dedicated. My special thanks to Peter Fallon, for his presence over the years and his invaluable attention to early drafts of this book. There are four other editors to whom I have, at different times, had reason to be grateful: Mick Imlah (1956–2009), Dillon Johnston, Jeff Holdridge and Christian Wiman.

Versions of these poems first appeared first in: *Best Irish Poetry* 2009 *Best Irish Poetry* 2010, *Blackbox Manifold*, *The Edinburgh Review*, *The Forward Book of Poetry* 2010, *The Irish Times*, *The Manchester Review*, *The Michigan Quarterly Review*, *The New European Poets* (Graywolf Press, 2008), *Poetry* ("In Praise of Sprinklers", "Swell", "Three Six Five Zero", "January Drought", "Game Night" and "The Unfaithful Housewife"), *Poetry Daily*, *Poetry Ireland Review*, *Poetry Review*, *The Sheffield Anthology: Poems from the City Imagined*, *Southword*, and *Sunday Miscellany* (RTE Radio).